My Catholic School Holiday Activity Book

Reproducible Sheets for Home and School

Written and Illustrated by Jennifer Galvin

Paulist Press

New York/Mahwah, N.J.

D1468424

For Kim and Shannon—who always support me one hundred percent.

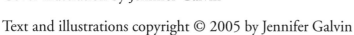
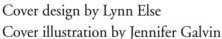

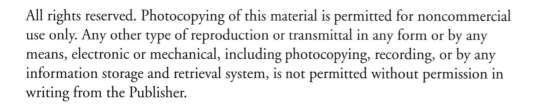

Cover design by Lynn Else
Cover illustration by Jennifer Galvin

Text and illustrations copyright © 2005 by Jennifer Galvin

The scripture quotations contained herein are from, or adapted from, the New Revised Standard Version Bible, copyright © 1989 by the Division of Christian Education of the National Council of the Churches of Christ in the U.S.A. and are used by permission. All rights reserved.

ISBN: 0-8091-6724-7

Published by Paulist Press
997 Macarthur Boulevard
Mahwah, New Jersey 07430

www.paulistpress.com

Printed and bound in the United States of America.

An Autumn Full of Friendship

God brings us special things to enjoy in nature each season. Color by number to find out one of the many beautiful ways God decorates the Earth in fall. Then write what friendship means to you inside your fall treasure, cut it out, and use it to start a class mural. Place a tree on a hill of grass and decorate it with your friendship treasures. At the beginning of each season, add to your mural to create a celebration of God's glory. Turn to the answer key for more directions.

1=Brown 2=Red 3=Orange 4=Leave blank

Back-to-School Word Find

Learning and learning about God are important jobs for students. When students go back to school, they need lots of supplies to make sure they are ready to reach for the stars, dream big, and learn. Find and circle all of the school supplies listed below. Your teacher can use this list for your back-to-school shopping. Add other supplies you need on the lines provided.

```
Z P E N C I L S W S R T Q R S
S C I S R O S F Z W R E S C I
G G S S C R U L O S C R P Q C
Z G L U C Q R S Z L T A Z R R
G L U G C I L R M N D S Q N A
L U L E Z Z S O N Z L E R N Y
E E R Z P Q R S T S D R R N O
A R S T N D W A O D N N Z R N
R U L E R R U R Z R Q N D W S
N Z R S P W W Y T H S S R Z Y
Q L O V E Z S R R N R B M T N
B I B L T R M N O T E B O O K
N R B I B R N N Z R N P A A R
C I R M A R K E R S S N R B Q
B I B C B C Q Y L P A P E R Q
```

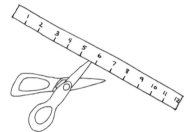

Bible	Glue	Pencils
Crayons	Markers	Rosary
Eraser	Notebook	Ruler
Folder	Paper	Scissors

_____
_____
_____
_____

Bonus—Can you find the words **love**, **to**, and **learn** in the word find?

St. Thérèse of Lisieux

St. Thérèse wanted to help people and love God through many "little ways." Her feast day is October 1. To find out St. Thérèse's special nickname, follow the line from each flower to a box, and put the letter from that flower in the box.

St. Francis of Assisi

We celebrate the feast of St. Francis on October 4. St. Francis is the patron saint of animals, ecologists, and merchants. He preached of a brotherhood among all living things. St. Francis still provides a wonderful role model for us today. As we celebrate his feast day this year, try to do an act of kindness for someone.

Find all sixteen things that are different in the second picture.

All Saints' Day

All Saints' Day is a holy day of obligation. On All Saints' Day, we celebrate all the saints, especially those that have no other feast day or may be known only to God. Celebrate All Saints' Day by going to Mass with your family and looking up a special saint that you want to learn more about.

Across

2. We honor _ _ _ _ _ _ on All Saints' Day.
4. All Saint's Day is a holy day of _ _ _ _ _ _ _ _ _ _ _.
6. We celebrate All Saints' Day by going to _ _ _ _.
7. All Saints' Day is celebrated on _ _ _ _ _ _ _ _ 1st.
8. All Saints' Day was originally celebrated in spring on _ _ _ 13th.

Down

1. The vigil for All Saints' Day is celebrated on October 31. Hallow means holy, so this day used to be called All Hallow's Eve. Today it is known as _ _ _ _ _ _ _ _ _.
3. All Saints' Day has been celebrated for over one _ _ _ _ _ _ _ _ years, a millennium!
5. All Saints' Day started as the _ _ _ _ _ of All Martyrs in the 4th century.
6. In the early eighth century, Pope Gregory III made All Saints' Day a feast day for all saints, not just _ _ _ _ _ _ _ _.

All Souls' Day

All Souls' Day is the day after All Saints' Day. On this special day, we remember loved ones and friends that have passed away. The feast day is based on a centuries-old celebration called the Festival of the Dead, in which families set out a meal for these loved ones to show they are still remembered. Different countries have different ways of observing this day. Match the word or phrase on the left with the description on the right to find out more.

November 2

All Souls' Day is sometimes also called this, especially in Mexico.

Candles

What is left empty at the table on All Souls' Day.

A Meal

Placed in windows on All Souls' Day in memory of those who have passed away.

Prayers

What is set out on the table on All Souls' Day in memory of those who have died.

Day of the Dead

The day the feast of All Souls' Day is usually celebrated.

An empty seat

How we can help our loved ones and friends that have passed away and are now in purgatory.

Election Day Maze

When there is a national election, Election Day is the first Tuesday after the first Monday in November. Local elections are held at other times as well. On Election Day, pray for our leaders and the important work they do for our country. Now, help these children wind their way through the maze to the voting box to vote in their school election.

Thanksgiving Psalm

Thanksgiving is a time when we remember to thank God for all the wonderful things in our lives. Leave the L, cross out the Y, then continue to cross out every other letter. Then write down the letters you have left in order on the blanks below. The psalm that is revealed will bring Thanksgiving thoughts and prayers into your heart. If you need help, refer to the psalm in your Bible.

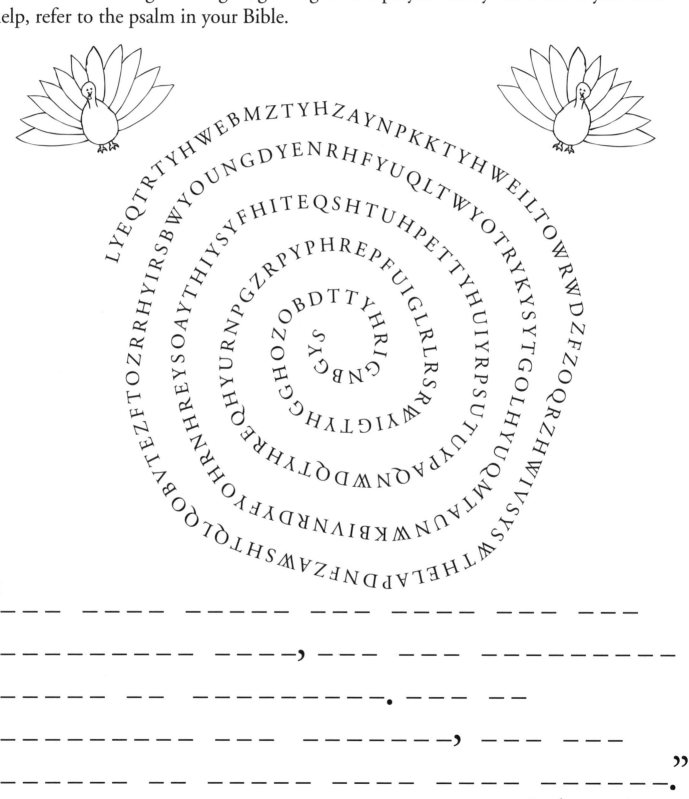

"
___ ___ ___ ___ ___ ___ ___ ___

_____ ___, ___ ___ _____ ___

____ __ _____. ___ __

_____ ___ _____, ___ ___ _

_____ __ _____ __ _____.
"

Psalms 107:8–9

Christ the King Dot-to-Dot

The feast of Christ the King is celebrated the last Sunday before the first Sunday of Advent. We celebrate Jesus Christ ruling our lives, not only in heaven, but here on earth as well. Say an Our Father, take Christ into your heart, and make him the King there. Do the dot-to-dot to find out what Christ the King might wear as he rules our lives. Then color the results.

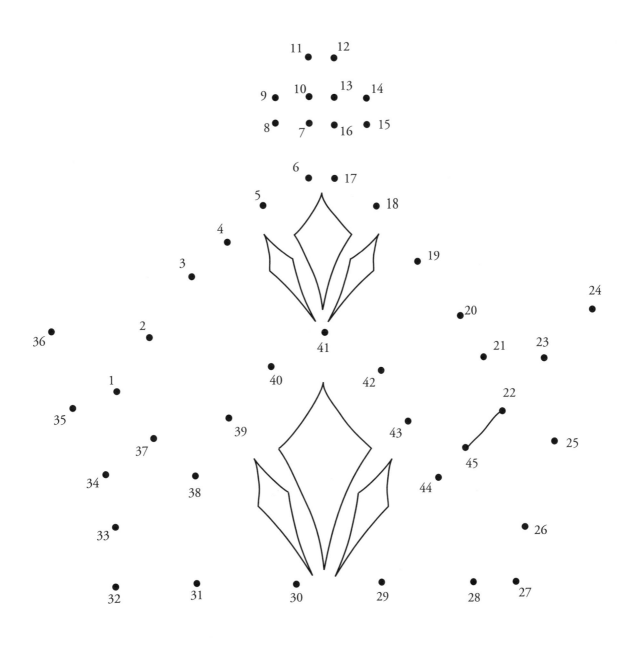

Christ the King might wear a _____.

Our Lady of Guadalupe

Our Lady of Guadalupe is the patron saint of Mexico and the Americas. When missionaries were trying to convert people to Catholicism, it wasn't easy. Then the Virgin Mary, appearing as a beautiful Aztec princess, appeared to Juan Diego, a poor Aztec Indian. She performed several miracles to convince the local bishop to allow a church for her to be built. Match the word or phrase on the left with the description on the right to find out more.

Saint Juan Diego

Miraculously appeared on some bushes as a sign for Juan Diego.

December 12

What Our Lady of Guadalupe wanted built where she appeared to Juan Diego.

A church

Patroness of Mexico and the Americas.

Roses

The day the Virgin Mary appeared to Juan Diego the first time.

Our Lady of Guadalupe

What appeared on the inside of the cloak when Juan Diego presented the bishop with the roses.

December 9, 1531

The day the feast of Our Lady of Guadalupe is celebrated in America.

Image of Mary

The person that the Virgin Mary appeared to in Mexico as Our Lady of Guadalupe.

Winter Wonderland

Another beautiful way God decorates the earth is with snow. Winter starts every year between December 21 and 23. Do the math problems inside the snowflake to help you crack the code. Then use the answers to fill in the blanks at the center of the snowflake and the bottom of the page. Decorate and cut out your snowflakes, then add them to your mural. Perhaps you can even add some glitter!

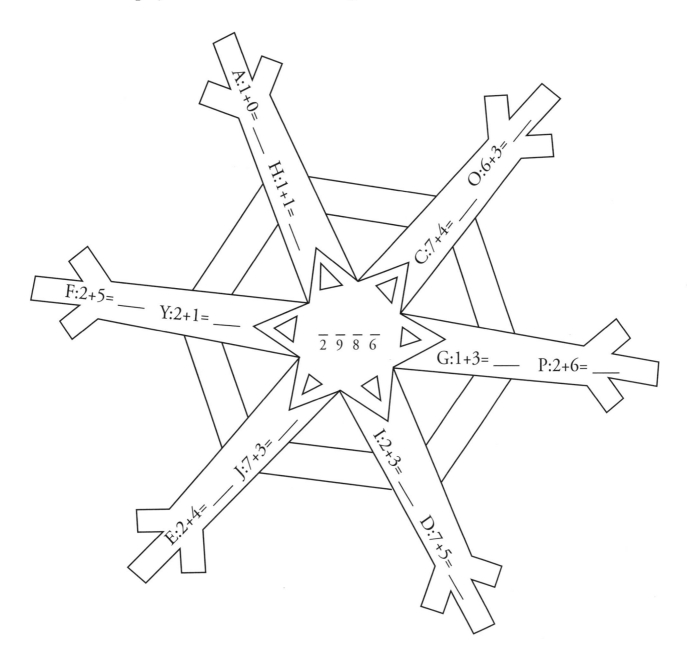

God gives us a winter full of _ _ _ _.
2 9 8 6

Christmas Day

Christmas is the day we celebrate the birth of Jesus Christ, the Son of God. Find out more about Christmas and Jesus by doing this crossword puzzle.

Across

3. Christmas Day is celebrated on the 25th day of _ _ _ _ _ _ _ _.
5. Three _ _ _ _ _ visited Jesus after he was born and brought gifts of gold, frankincense, and myrrh.
8. On Christmas Day we celebrate the birth of our Lord, _ _ _ _ _ Christ.
9. While shepherds were tending their sheep, _ _ _ _ _ _ appeared in the sky to tell them about Jesus' birth.

Down

1. Christmas is celebrated after the season of _ _ _ _ _ _.
2. Jesus was born in the town of _ _ _ _ _ _ _ _ _.
4. After Jesus was born, Mary laid him in a _ _ _ _ _ _.
6. The night before Jesus was born, there was no room at the inn, so he was born in a _ _ _ _ _ _.
7. A bright _ _ _ _ was shining in the sky above Bethlehem the night Jesus was born.

Rainbow of Diversity

We celebrate the birthday of the Reverend Martin Luther King Jr. on the third Monday in January. Martin Luther King Jr. was a famous African American leader. He preached the Gospel and dreamed of equality, peace, and freedom for all people. All people deserve kindness and respect. After you color this picture, write something about yourself that makes you special in each stripe of the rainbow.

The Hundredth Day

Many schools celebrate the hundredth day of school as a special day. It helps us learn to count up to one hundred. Celebrate each day of school by keeping God close to your heart. Perhaps you can pray the Our Father or do a small good deed every day until you reach 100. Here are 100 candies to help you with your counting. Connect the candies that look like this 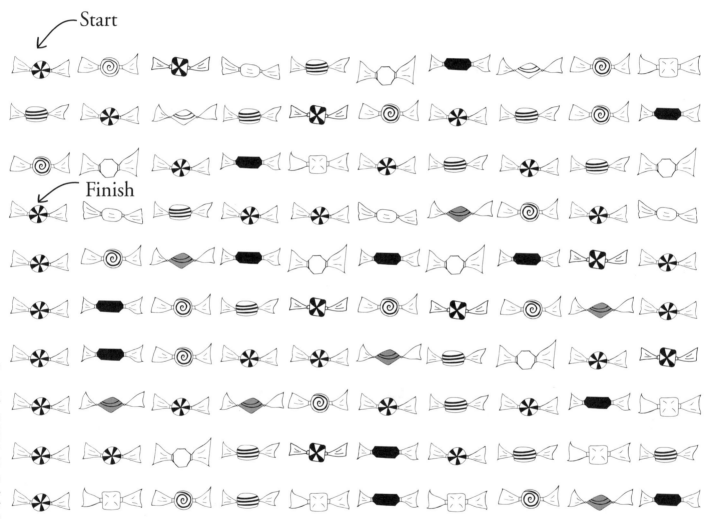 to find your way through the candies to the finish.

There is a design in the candy maze above. After you are done following the candies through the maze, look closely, then fill in the following sentence.

The early Christians used the sign of the _ _ _ _ to show that they were Christians.

Valentine's Day Matching

Valentine's Day is celebrated on February 14. Until 1969, Valentine's Day was an official feast day for three St. Valentines, all of whom were martyrs. It is no longer an official feast day, although it is still a major holiday and is celebrated widely. We celebrate love and friendship on Valentine's Day because long ago people believed February 14 was the day that birds paired off to build their nests. Three of the valentines below are exactly alike. Find and circle them. Then color all of the valentines.

Presentation of the Lord

Below is the story of the Presentation of our Lord as told in Luke. We celebrate the Presentation of the Lord on February 2. Read the story, then find the words in the passage that are in **bold** print.

```
S P I R S S P I R I T S L L S P P
J J S P I R G E N L O R R O O P R
C C E E R P R A I S E D R O E E
H H J S G R P R G N S R D D D A S
M M O S U R R G G N N P L R D C E
M G L S R S R E J O S G H I C E N
A B C D E C B N I S R F G H G N T
R B Y G Y N R T N R L M C P R H A
Y C J R L D A I M M A S T E R R T
G L O R L V J L M L S C T R C B I
R L V B L B J E J O S T L L M A O
G L B A L V O S R B D C E H R Z N
Q C S T A V S J L M Z A D M J T R
R C S V B Z E R B N R F N L P B D
Z R C D M R P M A S T T R V B L J
R G O D M N H H I J K M R P H N E
V M N C D M R N C M N W O R D C D
```

Guided by the **spirit**, Simeon came into the **temple**; and when **Mary** and **Joseph** brought in the child **Jesus**, Simeon took him in his arms and **praised God**, saying, "**Master**, now you are dismissing your servant in **peace**, according to your **word**; for my eyes have seen your **salvation**, which you have prepared in the presence of all peoples, a **light** for revelation to the **Gentiles** and for **glory** to your people **Israel**." Luke 2:27–32 (adapted)

Bonus—Can you find the words **Presentation**, **Lord**, and **chosen**?

Presidents' Day

We honor past and present United States presidents on Presidents' Day, the third Monday in February. Presidents' Day is celebrated in February because George Washington's and Abraham Lincoln's birthdays both occur in February. Color by number to reveal the silhouettes of two famous presidents.

1=red   2=white   3=blue   4=black

_____ and _____ are the two presidents whose silhouettes are in the picture.

19

St. Patrick's Day Dot-to-Dot

March 17 is the feast day of St. Patrick. St. Patrick is the patron saint of Ireland. He taught people about the Trinity, three persons in one God, using what is pictured in this dot-to-dot. Do the dot-to-dot to find out what St. Patrick used.

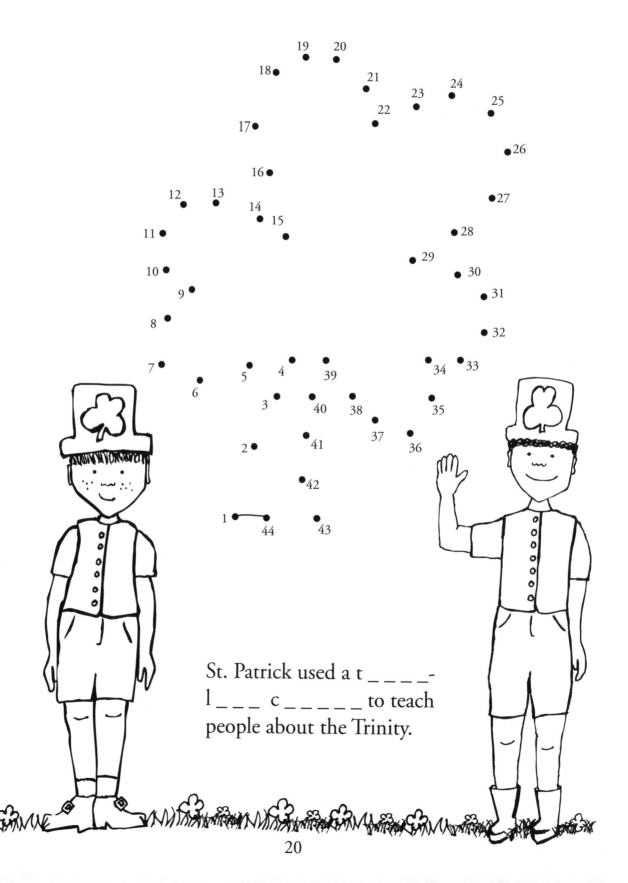

St. Patrick used a t _ _ _ _ -
l _ _ _ c _ _ _ _ _ to teach
people about the Trinity.

Feast of St. Joseph

We celebrate the feast of St. Joseph on March 19. St. Joseph was Jesus' foster father. St. Joseph is the patron saint of workers, fathers, and carpenters. Joseph was a carpenter and probably taught Jesus about carpentry when he was a boy. Color this picture of Joseph teaching Jesus carpentry.

Spring Splendor

Beautiful trees and flowers bloom in spring as God shows us new beginnings. Spring begins on March 20 or 21, depending on the year. Fill in the blanks inside each petal to help you crack the code. Then use the code numbers to fill in the blanks at the center of the flower and the bottom of the page. Decorate, cut out, and add your flower to your mural. You may want to create a green stem and leaf for your flower out of green construction paper.

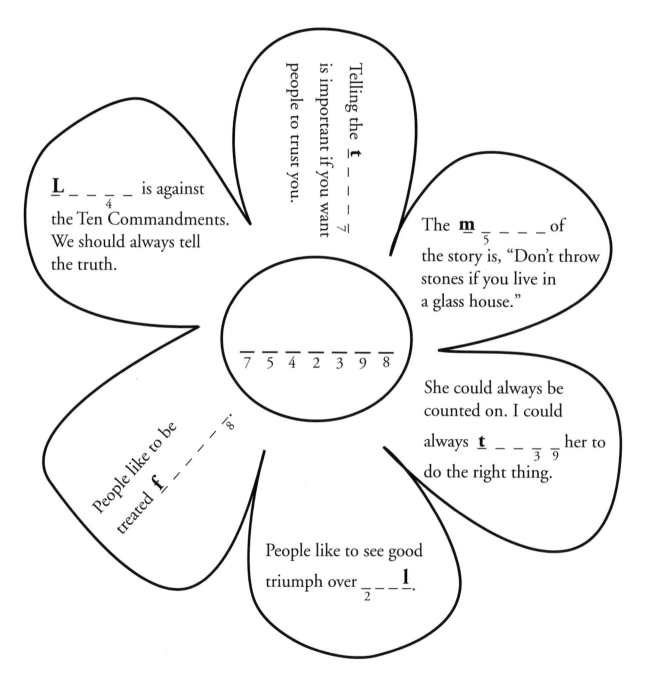

L _ _ _4_ is against the Ten Commandments. We should always tell the truth.

Telling the t_1_ _ _ _ _7 is important if you want people to trust you.

The m_5_ _ _ _ of the story is, "Don't throw stones if you live in a glass house."

People like to be treated f_ _ _ _ _ _8.

She could always be counted on. I could always t_ _ _3_9 her to do the right thing.

People like to see good triumph over _2_ _ _1.

Center: _7 _5 _4 _2 _3 _9 _8

God wants us to have a life full of _7 _5 _4 _2 _3 _9 _8.

Earth Day

On Earth Day, we celebrate God's gift of the Earth to us. We celebrate by remembering how we can take care of the Earth that God gave us. What's wrong with this picture? Hint: The kids forgot to clean up their playground for Earth Day. Find and circle 21 things that should have gone in the trash or recycling bin. Then color the picture.

Easter

Easter Sunday is the day we remember that Jesus died on the cross and rose from the dead to bring us eternal life with God after we die. The butterfly, the empty cross, and the egg are all Easter symbols of new life.

Find all seventeen things that are different in the second picture.

Mother's Day Maze

"Honor your father and your mother" from Exodus 20:12 reminds us to appreciate Mom on Mother's Day and every day. Help all the children take flowers to their mothers for Mother's Day. Follow the maze to the mothers, making sure not to step on any flowers on the way.

Crowning a Statue in May

In May we honor a very special person by crowning her statue with flowers. What is the name of the person whose statue we crown?

To find the answer, use the chart below to find which letter goes in each blank. Follow the first flower across and the second flower up to find each letter. Put the letters above the blanks at the bottom of the page.

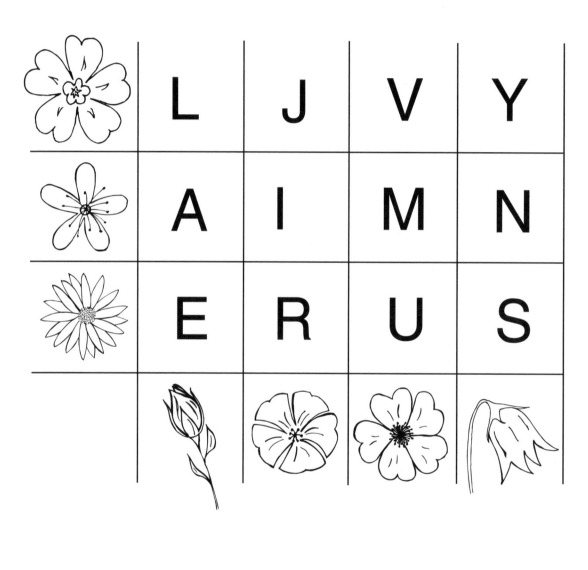

We honor _____ _____ _____ _____

Trinity Sunday

On Trinity Sunday we honor the most Holy Trinity. We worship one God, yet our God is three in one—the Father, the Son, and the Holy Spirit.

Unscramble these words to find out more about the Holy Trinity.

1. Trinity Sunday is the first _ _ _ _ _ _ NYDAUS after Pentecost.

2. Trinity Sunday honors the Most Holy _ _ _ _ _ _ _.YRTTIIN

3. The Trinity is made up of the Father, the _ _ _ NSO, and the Holy Spirit.

4. We believe in the Trinity, God in three persons, because of our _ _ _ _ _ THAFI in God.

5. Jesus speaks of the Holy Trinity in this Bible verse: "Go therefore and make disciples of all nations, baptizing them in the name of the _ _ _ _ _ _ THAEFR and of the Son and of the Holy Spirit." Matthew 28:19

6. The Holy Spirit was sent by Jesus to be with us in our _ _ _ _ _ _.TSAERH

7. God the Father is the _ _ _ _ _ _ _ TEAORRC of Heaven and Earth.

8. Jesus the Son died on the _ _ _ _ _ OCSSR to save us from our sins.

Corpus Christi

On the feast of Corpus Christi, we take time to appreciate a special sacrament. This feast is also known as the feast of the Body of Christ. Crack the code and fill in the blanks below to find out what sacrament we honor on the feast of Corpus Christi.

A:___=4-2   H:___=6-5   O:___=12-2   V:___=18-3
B:___=21-1   I:___=10-3   P:___=24-2   W:___=20-1
C:___=3-0   J:___=16-3   Q:___=26-1   X:___=19-3
D:___=9-5   K:___=24-0   R:___=14-2   Y:___=26-0
E:___=9-3   L:___=8-3   S:___=10-1   Z:___=19-2
F:___=12-1   M:___=20-2   T:___=9-1
G:___=23-2   N:___=26-3   U:___=16-2

$$\overline{}\ \overline{}\ \overline{}\quad \overline{}\ \overline{}\ \overline{}\ \overline{}$$
$$\ \ 8\quad 1\quad 6\qquad 1\quad 10\quad 5\quad 26$$

$$\overline{}\ \overline{}\ \overline{}\ \overline{}\ \overline{}\ \overline{}\ \overline{}\ \overline{}\ \overline{}$$
$$6\quad 14\quad 3\quad 1\quad 2\quad 12\quad 7\quad 9\quad 8$$

Copyright © 2005, My Catholic School Holiday Activity Book. Published by Paulist Press.

Father's Day

"Children, obey your parents in the Lord, for this is right. 'Honor your father and mother.' This is the first commandment with a promise: 'Honor your parents so your own life will be good and you may live long on the earth.'" Ephesians 6:1-3 (adapted)

Color this Father's Day picture to remind you to appreciate both your father and your Heavenly Father and all they do for you.

A Summer Full of Dreams

God has filled summer with joyful colors and warmth for us to enjoy. As you play this summer, find a special place in your heart to remember God. Think of a marvelous dream to help make God's world a better place. Then, color by number to find a summer surprise for your mural. Cut it out, write your dream in the middle, and hang it on your seasons mural. Your four seasons mural now celebrates a whole year full of friendship, hope, honesty, and dreams!

1=Purple 2=Blue 3=Green 4=White 5=Leave blank

Answers

Page 3
A finished mural could look something like this.

Page 4
```
Z P E N C I L S W S R T Q R S
S C I S R O S F Z W R E S C I
G G S S C R U L O S C R P Q C
Z G L U C O R S Z L T A Z R R
G L U G C I L R M N D S Q N A
L U L E Z Z S O N Z L E R N Y
E E R Z P Q R S T S D R R N O
A R S T N D W A O D N N Z R N
R U L E R R U R Z R Q N D W S
N Z R S P W W Y T H S S R Z Y
Q L O V E Z S R R N R B M N
B I B L T R M N O T E B O O K
N R B I B R N N Z R N P A A R
C I R M A R K E R S S N R B Q
B Y B C B C Q Y L P A P E R Q
```

Page 5
"THE LITTLE FLOWER"

Page 6

Page 7
1. H
2. SAINTS
3. THOU
4. OBLIGATION
5. F
6. MASS
7. NOVEMBER
8. MARTYRS
HALLOWEEN
THOUSAND
FEAST

Page 8
November 2 — The day the feast of All Souls' Day is usually celebrated.

Candles — Placed in windows on All Souls' Day in memory of those who have passed away.

A Meal — What is set out on the table on All Souls' Day in memory of those who have died.

Prayers — How we can help our loved ones and friends that have passed away and are now in purgatory.

Day of the Dead — All Souls' Day is sometimes also called this, especially in Mexico.

An empty seat — What is left empty at the table on All Souls' Day.

Page 9

Page 10
"LET THEM THANK THE LORD FOR HIS STEADFAST LOVE, FOR HIS WONDERFUL WORKS TO HUMANKIND FOR HE SATISFIES THE THIRSTY, AND THE HUNGRY HE FILLS WITH GOOD THINGS."
—Psalm 107:8–9

Page 11
Christ the King might wear a CROWN.

Page 12
Saint Juan Diego — The person that the Virgin Mary appeared to in Mexico as Our Lady of Guadalupe.

December 12 — The day the feast of Our Lady of Guadalupe is celebrated in America.

A church — What Our Lady of Guadalupe wanted built where she appeared to Juan Diego.

Roses — Miraculously appeared on some bushes as a sign for Juan Diego.

Our Lady of Guadalupe — Patroness of Mexico and the Americas.

December 9, 1531 — The day the Virgin Mary appeared to Juan Diego the first time.

Image of Mary — What appeared on the inside of the cloak when Juan Diego presented the bishop with the roses.

Page 13
A:1+0= 1 H:1+1= 2 G:7+4= 11 O:6+3= 9
E:2+5= 7 Y:2+1= 3
P:2+6= 8
G:1+3= 4
E:2+4= 6 J:7+3= 10
I:2+3= 5 D:7+5= 12
HOPE 2986

God gives us a winter full of H O P E.
2 9 8 6

Page 14
1. A
2. B
3. DECEMBER
4. MANGER
5. KING
6. STABLE
7. STAR
8. JESUS
9. ANGELS
ADVENT
BETHLEHEM

31

Answers

Page 16

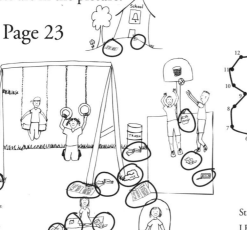

Start

Finish

The early Christians used the sign of the **FISH** to show that they were Christians.

Page 18

WASHINGTON and LINCOLN are the two presidents whose silhouettes are in the picture.

Page 17

Page 19

```
S P I R S S P I R I T S L L S P P
J O S P I R G E N L O R R O O P R
C E E E R P R A I S E D R O E E
H H J S G R P R G N S R D D D R
M M O S U R R G G N N O S G I C E
M G L S R S R E J O S G H I C E N
A B C D E C B N I S R F G H G N T
R B Y G Y N R T N R I M C P R H A
V C J R L D A I M A S T E R R T
G L O R L V J L M L S C T R C B I
R L V B L B J E J O S T L D M A O
G L B A L V O S R B D C E H R Z N
Q C S T A V S J L M Z A D M J T R
R C S V B Z E R B N R F N L P B D
Z R C D M R P M A S T T R V B L J
R G O D M N H H I J K M R P H N E
V M N C D M R N C M N W O R D C D
```

Page 20

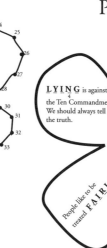

St. Patrick used a THREE-LEAF CLOVER to teach people about the Trinity.

Page 22

Telling the **TRUTH** is important if you want people to trust you.

LYING is against the Ten Commandments. We should always tell the truth.

The **MORAL** of the story is, "Don't throw stones if you live in a glass house."

HONESTY

She could always be counted on. I could always **TRUST** her to do the right thing.

People like to be treated **FAIRLY**.

People like to see good triumph over **EVIL**.

God wants us to have a life full of **HONESTY**.

Page 23

Page 24

Page 25

Page 25

Page 26

We honor **MARY**

Page 27

1. Trinity Sunday is the first SUNDAY after Pentecost.
2. Trinity Sunday honors the Most Holy TRINITY.
3. The Trinity is made up of the Father, the SON, and the Holy Spirit.
4. We believe in the Trinity, God in three persons, because of our FAITH in God.
5. Jesus speaks of the Holy Trinity in this Bible verse: "Go therefore and make disciples of all nations, baptizing them in the name of the FATHER and of the Son and of the Holy Spirit." Matthew 28:19
6. The Holy Spirit was sent by Jesus to be with us in our HEARTS.
7. God, the Father, is the CREATOR of Heaven and Earth.
8. Jesus, the Son, died on the CROSS to save us from our sins.

Page 28

A: 2 =4-2
B: 20 =21-1
C: 3 =3-0
D: 4 =9-5
E: 6 =9-3
F: 11 =12-1
G: 21 =23-2
H: 1 =6-5
I: 7 =10-3
J: 13 =16-3
K: 24 =24-0
L: 5 =8-3
M: 18 =20-2
N: 23 =26-3
O: 10 =12-2
P: 22 =24-2
Q: 25 =26-1
R: 12 =14-2
S: 9 =10-1
T: 8 =9-1
U: 14 =16-2
V: 15 =18-3
W: 19 =20-1
X: 16 =19-3
Y: 26 =26-0
Z: 17 =19-2

THE HOLY
8 1 6 1 10 5 26
EUCHARIST
6 14 3 1 2 12 7 9 8